# Gratitude

## GROW & CHANGE YOUR WORLD
## ONE THANK YOU AT A TIME

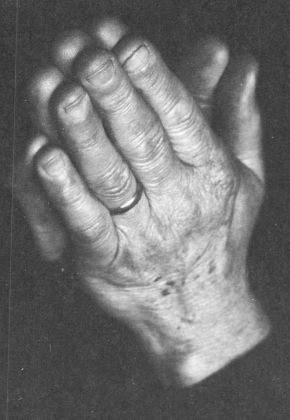

RAJESH SETTY

# Table of Contents

# Advance Praise
(in alphabetical order)

"Gratitude is the social glue that connects hands and hearts, and minds together. As our world continues to expand globally gratitude is a human language that crosses all borders, ages and perceived divisions. In this book Rajesh captures the essence and simplicity of gratitude. I write one hand written thank you note each day. As a result my life is more fulfilling, my relationships stronger and joy fills my heart in new and ever expanding ways. Don't just read this book, apply the actions prescribed each day and make meaningful change in your life and the lives of those around you.

Thank you Rajesh for this opportunity to be a part of your work!"

*- Holly Duckworth*
*CEO, Leadership Solutions International*

"Share your gratitude with someone, anyone, today. Tomorrow is too far away and yesterday is gone. Words of gratitude translate through languages and soften the borders that separate us. When you tell someone - a family member, a friend, a colleague or a customer - you are grateful, you'll see the relationship deepen. **Want to experience a better, more grateful life? In this book, Rajesh Setty shows you how.**"

*- Jason W. Womack*
*Author of "Your Best Just Got Better:*
*a leader's guide to productivity"*

---

"The arrival of the Age of Social means that everything about business is fundamentally changing. How you market, sell, service and more. Building genuine relationships is not a buzzword or a catchphrase, it's mission critical and expressing gratitude to those in your community is a key step in that process. Few understand the dynamics as well- or more sincerely- than Rajesh Setty. Now, buy the book. You can thank me later! ;-)"

*- Jeremy Epstein*
*VP of Marketing, Sprinklr*

---

"Just like hedonic highs are short-lived we can quickly get habituated to others' act of helpfulness and begin to take generous people for granted. If you, too, have felt slighted by such occurrences, you too, may want to get actionable insights from wise Rajesh Setty on how to ensure that you show genuine gratitude to others. Then, together, we can be models for the appreciative behavior we value and deepen our relationships in mutually enriching ways. Perhaps we can even scale the spirit of generosity"

*- Kare Anderson*
*Author of Moving From Me to We and Mutuality Matters*

"If you want to be significant you need to impact others. Rajesh Setty gives you the exact blueprint in his powerful and liberating book, " Gratitude." Without this concise and effective action plan, you will miss a compelling opportunity to leverage your impact in the world. If you execute this exciting action plan now, you will be grateful for a lifetime."

*- Ken McArthur*
*Best-Selling Author of "Impact: How to Get Noticed, Motivate*
*Millions and Make a Difference in a Noisy World."*

---

Rajesh Setty has been writing for many years... and like vintage wine, his writing just grows richer and deeper as it ages!

In "Gratitude", he touches greater heights than ever before, translating a universal truth into a pragmatic practice that touches lives and improves relationships.

My career as a pediatric heart surgeon treating children dealt with a bad hand by nature has helped me deeply appreciate many of the "small things" that many take for granted - like a child's healthy, happy smile. Living an "attitude of gratitude" has transformed many facets of my life deeply, magically.

"Gratitude" deconstructs the mystery of being constantly in this state of gratefulness and provides a simple, practical road map anyone can follow.

At the end of this short, sweet read, I'm sure you'll also be nodding in agreement with the core premise... "Yes, there is joy in giving and joy in grateful living."

*- Dr.Mani Sivasubramanian*
*Heart surgeon and Writer*

"Want to change a bad attitude in others and yourself in an instant? You can't feel gratitude and (a bad) attitude at the same time. Go ahead, try it. Then take it one step further and thank a person and it will brighter your and their day. And if you want to turn a taste of this into a full course meal and fuller life, buy Rajesh Setty's wonderful book."

*- Mark Goulston*
*Author of "Just Listen" Discover the Secret to Getting Through to Absolutely Anyone and Co-Founder, Heartfelt Leadership."*

---

There is an old adage that says you should give without expecting. While this still applies, if you are a recipient of someone's generosity, you need to take the responsibility to acknowledge, appreciate and thank the giver. That is the essence of this book and it delivers. Raj masterfully weaves in engaging anecdotes to make his points and also gets the reader to practice and take action. A practical and generous book indeed."

*- MR Rangaswami*
*Publisher SandHill.com and Founder of Indiaspora*

---

"Reflect, respond, release, reward, rejoice, reframe. These six words change the gratitude game forever. Rajesh Setty gives us the master blueprint to give with gratitude and to live with gratitude. Big doors swing on little hinges. You'll find many little hinges that will open up big doors of gratitude. Grab this book, read it, and read it again. It will change your life. It has mine. Thank you Rajesh. I am grateful to you for sharing this simple, profound wisdom."

*- Mitch Axelrod*
*Author of The New Game of Selling*

"This book is one of the greatest gifts you can receive. Applying Rajesh's message of "practical generosity" will dramatically impact your life for good and empower you to influence the lives of those around you. Receive this transformational teaching with open arms and watch your life flourish."

*- Richie Norton*
*Bestselling author of The Power of Starting Something Stupid*

---

"Gratitude is an amazing force to own and share. No one explains it as beautifully as Rajesh Setty in this highly worthy book which is sure to leave you asking for more. To fully experience Rajesh's craftsmanship as a "masterful writer", you would really have to immerse yourself in the sheer simplicity and elegance of his words that weave core tenets of Sociology, Psychology, and Anthropology together to present what I think is an absolute masterpiece. There's a deep sense of old school spirituality combed with new school tenacity here. Quintessential Rajesh, I say!"

*- Rohan Chandrashekar*
*Founder and CEO, BuzzValve.*

---

"For many people the concept of gratitude becomes an intellectual exercise, and not truly a practice. What Rajesh has done with this book give us an actionable way to turn gratitude into a daily habit. It becomes something you do and eventually who you are."

*- Srinivas Rao*
*Host of The Unmistakable Creative Podcast and*
*Author of The Art of Being Unmistakable..*

"As I am reading your book on gratitude, I find myself singing the words to Jimmy Buffett's song, Attitude of Gratitude, laughing to and at myself, feeling joy and appreciation for all the blessings in my life. I give thanks to you my friend and I am grateful for the wise and loving gifts you unconditionally give to me."

*- Stuart Rudick*
*Partner at Mindfull Investors*

---

"We often take for granted the very things that most deserve, our gratitude. As I started to read Rajesh Setty's brilliant book on gratitude, I was immediately reminded of the power of being thankful and kind. Gratitude is truly a personal and business force multiplier. Setty demonstrates examples of practicing the art of gratitude and in a simple and meaningful way reminds us that positive people can and do achieve more. I highly recommend 'Gratitude Frequency' to business executives, entrepreneurs and students of leadership and management. I plan to give a copy to all of my directors and managers."

*- Vala Afshar*
*CMO of Extreme Networks*

# Acknowledgements

"This book adventure was no different than any of my other projects – I got a lot of help from a number of my friends to bring this idea to a reality.

My attempt to list everyone will be flawed, as I am sure I will miss a few. With that disclaimer, here are my thanks to the following people (in alphabetical order)

Arun Nithyanandam | Brainstorming on the title and strategy for the book

Clay Hebert | Ideas on crowdfunding especially the video script

Japjot Sethi | Supporting the project in more than one way"

Jason Franzen | For bringing his magic to the thank you cards

Kate Neschke | Multiple editing rounds of the book

Nilesh Kapse | Design, print and production with care

Rohit Nallapeta | Supporting the project in more than one way

Sachit Gupta | Strategy and execution for the book's online presence

Srinivas N Jay | For pouring his heart into bringing thoughtful cards alive

And, special thanks to the following people, I respect, who took the time to read the book in advance and provide a testimonial to support the project:

Holly Duckworth, Jason W. Womack, Jeremy Epstein, Kare Anderson, Ken McArthur, Mani Sivasubramaniam, Mark Goulston, MR Rangaswami, Mitch Axelrod, Richie Norton, Rohan Chandrashekar, Srinivas Rao, Stuart Rudick and Vala Afshar.

Special thanks to Marshall Goldsmith for writing the foreword for the book.

Lastly to Kavitha and Sumukh who make my life very special.

Warmly,

Rajesh

# Foreword
Marshall Goldsmith

Most of us don't spend enough time in gratitude. Being grateful isn't an easy to state to be in – until you're in it and then you'll never want to leave!

In this beautiful book about attaining and maintaining a state of gratitude, Rajesh Setty teaches us who, what, where, when, and why to be grateful. He teaches us about saying, "Thank you". Thanking people is important because it expresses gratitude – one of our most basic emotions. Not an abstraction, it is a genuine emotion. You may expect someone to be grateful or someone may expect it of you, but you can't make yourself or someone else "feel grateful".

Yet, when someone does something nice for you, they expect gratitude and they think less of you for withholding it. Think about the last time you gave someone a gift. If they didn't say thank you, how did you feel about them?

When someone gives you a gift, you wouldn't say, "This is a bad gift!" You would say, "Thank you." If you can use the gift, use it. If you don't want to use it, put it in the closet and "let it go." This is the giving power of being grateful. It's not about the gift, it's about the care someone else has shown to you in their giving.

Being grateful works at work – in your efforts to become a better leader, team member, or co-worker.

And, it works at home – in your efforts to become a better friend or family member.

Get used to saying "Thank you". Get used to being grateful and accepting what is. Let Rajesh Setty teach you about gratitude, the how, the why, and the many different ways it will improve your life and relationships.

As Rajesh notes, some people think that being grateful, counting your blessings, can lead to complacency. I've noted in some of my works that the complex emotion of gratitude can be complicated to express and so sometimes can be interpreted as submissive behavior. I love Rajesh's simple counter to these negative opinions of being grateful. He says,

"Why should feeling blessed dampen your dreams? In fact, if you don't learn the art of having gratitude, when you reach your dreams you may not even see it. Your sights would simply be set on the new dream. This dream that you just achieved is taken for granted in a heartbeat."

"The bottom line is: if you can't feel blessed for what you already have, why spend your time chasing after what you don't have? Simply speaking, when you do finally get what you don't have, you are just feeding the never-ending quest for more without taking into account all the things that you already have and building a lifestyle and mindset of gratefulness."

"You can keep 'getting' new things but will you ever know how to truly appreciate them and be happy or content?"

I wholeheartedly agree. This is the "Great Western Disease" I talk about so frequently in my talks around the country. The Great Western Disease can be stated thus: "I'll be happy when?". I've learned, as Rajesh will teach you in this wonderful book, to be happy now. And the greatest tool in being happy now is gratitude.

I hope you take this to heart and learn all you can from Rajesh's wise words. You're going to need this knowledge as you travel the road to success in all you do.

Life is good.

Marshall Goldsmith

Marshall Goldsmith author or editor of 34 books including the global bestsellers *MOJO* and *What Got You Here Won't Get You There.*

# Why I Wrote This Book

I have been speaking on the topic of generosity lately. No, not the generosity of a charitable kind. I'm speaking of the **practical generosity** where you give a gift of your network, knowledge, mindshare and insights to move things forward on projects that matter most to the recipient. The Practical Generosity Quotient (PGQ) is **the ratio of "capacity added" to "capacity needed"** by someone to make something meaningful happen.

If "lip service" is on one end of the PGQ spectrum, high "practical generosity quotient" is on the other end of the spectrum.

My talks were being well received but the conversations I was having with attendees after I spoke finally led to the creation of this project.

Let me explain ...

Here is what happened.

> More than hundred people shared with me their personal stories of all kinds and levels of generosity.

> If I take a sample of ten people in the group, only two people admitted that they were the ones that had taken others for granted and felt that they wanted to do something to "fix" it by reaching out to those that they had taken for granted.

> The other eight shared their "silent hurt" about their earlier acts of generosity being taken for granted. They had made a significant impact yet felt that recipients of their generosity simply moved on without even acknowledgement or thanks. I started to pay attention to the feedback of people feeling "taken for granted" and realized that it was much more common than I had imagined.

> Overall, I realized that there are so many people walking with heavy hearts and feeling incomplete because they had the feeling of been taken for granted sometime in their past. Honestly, it was shocking to see some people who were carrying this baggage for two or three decades. Ouch!

> I really doubt that these eight people in the second group were looking for a profit share for the benefits that their contributions made. They were, in my opinion, looking for signs to show them **that their acts mattered in a positive way**. That would have given the necessary boost to continue or accelerate their generous acts rather than being "careful and guarded" about their next positive moves.

What was required was a positive ripple – something that will put the generosity engine back on track in a big way.

It could start with a simple thank you.

And, it could start with you.

In other words, this little book (with you taking action, of course) can start a ripple to get people to:

- **Reflect** on their past to see if they have taken people for granted.

- **Respond** by taking the small act of sending a "Thank You" note and start "fixing" whatever can be fixed.

- **Release** those who have taken them for granted by dropping any expectations of reciprocation.

- **Reward** themselves with the gift of time that was being robbed by the extra baggage they were carrying.

- **Rejoice** because they have relieved themselves from carrying guilt or expectation(s).

- **Reframe** the concept of gratitude to thank powerfully in the future.

This little book is my attempt to start the ripple and with your help, this ripple can become a wave and that wave can become a movement.

Without you taking action this book is incomplete.

Over to you!

# Introduction

This book is in your hands for a reason. You have a choice. You can read this as an intellectual entertainment exercise. Or you can read, reflect and act on some of the ideas presented here. I sincerely hope that you will choose the latter option.

First, remind yourself that you didn't reach where you are today all on your own. Your life is filled with hundreds of acts of generosity of various forms and levels.

Being the grateful recipient of those generous acts is not optional. You already know that. On the other hand, this is not something you do to simply fulfill your obligations. It is a way to elevate the level at which you live your life. It is a richer experience than what you get when you don't practice grateful living. The keyword here is **experience** - meaning you will "experience" the value of it when you practice grateful living.

While grateful living might start with a simple act of saying "Thank You" more often, the goal is to make it your second nature. Whenever you are not consciously making an effort to be thinking and acting in a grateful way out of a habit then it totally becomes a part of your life. The magic is when you feel it in your heart and soul beyond what you think in your mind.

Let us shift the attention for a minute to the other side – to those that are giving.

The first point here is about what it costs for someone to give.

> There is an old adage that **you should give without expecting**. This applies to most cases, especially when you are giving for a charity, but not when the act of giving comes at a significant cost to you. These acts of generosity definitely won't be sustainable if you are putting the interests of those that are depending on you because you want to feel good about giving. In other words, you have to give with a full heart but without shying away from your responsibilities and commitments. You can't break promises you made to the loved ones just because you feel good about giving.

The second point here is to remember that even the value of the gift may not diminish even when it costs only a little to give.

> A smarter approach would be to ggive and keep investing yourself in parallel so that you can give valuable gifts with low incremental costs to you. When you have the capacity and power, a tiny act can cause a big wave. For example, when Gary Vaynerchuk or Guy Kawasaki puts out a tweet about your project, it makes a BIG difference. It's a big gift that they showered on you. The incremental cost

to them was the time it took to share that tweet but the real cost to them is what investments they had to make to reach the state when a small incremental cost could create a huge wave.

With the above in the background, pay attention to the blind spot when it comes to being grateful.

You receive gifts every day. Sometimes, they are gifts that take a great deal of work for the other person to give and sometimes they're gifts that have a low incremental cost for the other person. It all depends on the power and capacity of the giver. Gratitude is about what and how much it means to you in value and not what the cost was to the giver.

Remember that there is joy in giving and there is joy in grateful living.

Let the journey begin.

# Shifting the Mindset

> *"At the age of 18, I made up my mind to never have another bad day in life. I dove into an endless sea of gratitude from which I've never emerged."*
>
> *- Patch Adams*

# Count Your Blessings Every Day

In India, thousands of kids are taught to follow the simple practice of saying thanks before every meal. The message to the kids is clear and simple:

**Close your eyes and thank GOD for providing that meal.**

I am sure similar kind of practice is replicated in many cultures across the world. It is a simple act of counting your blessings everyday. In our quest to go after what we don't have, we tend to completely forget and be grateful for what we already have.

I urge you to do this simple exercise. Take a look at the following list and for every item that applies to you, add a point to your score.

1. I don't have any physical handicaps.

2. I get at least two square meals everyday.

3. I have a family.

4. I have clean drinking water.

5. I have a college degree.

6. I have a job.

7. I have a car to get to work and leisure activities.

8. I have at least two close friends whom I trust.

9. I have a place to live, whether to rent or own.

10. I have a TV at home.

11. I have freedom of speech in the country I live.

12. I am afford to send my kids to school.

We can go on further but I guess you get the point. How many times have you said thanks for any of the things that you said yes to on the list above? Take a moment to notice how many things you took for granted without even thinking about it.

It may seem reasonable to follow the crowd and get caught in the 'busy' trap. Almost everyone around you is running like crazy to get what they don't have and seldom take time to be grateful for what they already have. Common sense says that if you follow the crowd, you can't expect to "stand out" from it.

I have encountered people who have a counterpoint to the "count your blessings everyday" approach.

Their main points against the approach are:

a) This will lead to complacency.

b) There won't be a motivation to stretch.

My point is that "counting your blessings everyday" has nothing to do with ambition or motivation. I don't think there is any connection to having the gratitude and 'feeling blessed' everyday with going after your dreams.

Of course, you can always connect seemingly unrelated things with your creativity.

Why should 'feeling blessed' dampen your dreams? In fact, if you don't learn the art of having gratitude, then, when you reach your dreams you may not even notice it. Your sights would be instantly set on a new dream. The dream that you just achieved is taken for granted in a heartbeat.

**The bottom line is:** if you can't feel blessed for what you already have, why spend your time chasing after what you don't have? Because, when you do finally get what you don't have, you are just feeding the never-ending quest for more without taking into account all the things that you already have and building a lifestyle and mindset of gratefulness.

You can keep "getting" new things but will you ever know how to truly appreciate them and be happy or content?

> "*When it comes to life, the critical thing is whether you take things for granted or take them with gratitude.*"

> — *Gilbert K. Chesterton*

# The Magic Counter

Here is a super simple exercise. I recommend doing at the end of the month but if you're in the middle of the month, you can do this for the previous month.

**The Exercise**

Take the total number of days in the month. Choose a random number between first and last day of the month. Take a piece of paper and make two columns. Column one "Thank You Given" and the other "Thank You Received."

Now go to your email Inbox for that day in the previous month.

First go through the sent items. Quickly browse through every single email and take note of whenever you feel there was a genuine, from the heart "Thank You" embedded within the email, add one to the "Thank You Given" column.

Next, go through the messages that were in your inbox for that day and do the same exercise. This time, add one to the "Thank You Received" column every time you see a genuine "Thank You" embedded within the received email.

Now, pick a "Thank You Baseline"; a number that you think is a reasonable number of "Thank You' given and received per month. For this exercise, let's assume that you picked a number seven.

**The Analysis**

Let's look at the "Thank You Given" column. If it is more than the baseline number, there is nothing to worry.

If the "Thank You Given" is less than the baseline number, you need to think about the reasons. There may be many reasons but two reasons are worth thinking about:

1. You don't have enough people surrounding you that you can be thankful for. This is not good.

2. You are not thanking the people enough for all the help that you are receiving from them. This is also not good.

Both require you to change something. Something for you to think about.

Next, let's look at the "Thank You Received" column. If it is less than the baseline number, there are many possibilities but there is an important one to remember:

You are not contributing enough that people are touched to take the time to send you a 'thank you' note. Not good.

This requires you to change something. Something else for you to think about.

Now, please don't get carried away by the specific method outlined. I wanted to present an exercise that is easy to implement to get you thinking in the right mindset. The concept behind this exercise is more important than the actual method.

The bottom line is that most people don't take the time to thank. Only you know whether you are like most people.

**Why?**

There could be many reasons, but usually people are just busy focusing on their own life. But, **you have the opportunity to not be like most people**. Every time you consume, take the time to see who was the provider and go out of the way to send them a 'thank you' note. It will likely make their day and in turn, they could be encouraged to pay the gratitude forward. If more people did this small act, a big difference could be made. Honestly, while most people are busy you are not like most people. Otherwise, you would not be reading this book.

Building the habit of gratitude really has one small question to ask:

**If you have the time to celebrate the gift you received, you MUST have the time to thank the giver for that gift. No exceptions.**

Remember that it may take you only a minute to send a heartfelt 'thank you' note but that act will make someone's day on the other end.

| Mon | Tue | Wed | Thu | Fri | Sat | Sun |
|-----|-----|-----|-----|-----|-----|-----|

.....to help you to grow everyday

> "*Gratitude is not only the greatest of virtues, but the parent of all others.*"
>
> *- Marcus Tullius Cicero*

# A Thank You a Day

A "Thank You" a day will do something magical. It will keep you growing everyday.

How will "A Thank You a Day" help you to grow everyday?

Here is how:

Think about it – for you to feel thankful everyday you have to be surrounded by people who contribute to your world. These people are those ones who will challenge and help you to become a "better you" every single day. You don't need any other reason to be thankful everyday.

Being thankful for those amazing people around you is important.

How about thinking the other way around?

Who should you be and what should you do so that someone around you feels thankful because you were one of those people in their network?

Living a life worthy of deserving a 'thank you' every day is not easy. For starters, you need to care beyond what is considered normal. Second, you have to act in a way that demonstrates your care. Third, for you to care and act in a way that demonstrates that care, you need the relevant knowledge, capacity and the right intent. With this setup you will have no choice but to keep growing.

It is never too late to make a pact to make a positive impact!

*one more*

"*If you want to be happy, practice compassion. If you want others to be happy, practice compassion*"

- *Dalai Lama*

# One More...

You might be asking, "Can one more 'thank you' really make that much of a difference?" The answer is yes. Just ask any person who received that last 'thank you' from you.

It seems so small, so why the focus on just "one more" thank you? The concept is so simple but one that has changed my life in a very profound way. Let's get right to the heart of it.

Since printing this page may not be easy, use a sheet of paper or a notebook to carry out this exercise.

Think about your most recent "win". A win could be anything that has moved the needle for you in a significant way. This might be a personal achievement, or a breakthrough in your career. It could even be something that made a real difference to your loved ones as well.

Now, think about the people who have played a part in that win. From mentors, parents and co-workers, to even people who might have played a small part as well. They are equally important. Let's use the worksheet below to write this down.

What was the win? (Write one or two lines.)

_____

_____

Who helped you get this win? (Write their name and contribution, adding more lines if necessary.)

1. _____

2. _____

3. _____

4. _____

5. _____

6. _____

7. _____

8. _____

9. _____

10. _____

Take as much time as required but the goal is to list everyone who helped you in any measure, large or small.

Once you have finished the list take another two minutes to think of anyone else whom you should add. It's important to record everyone who played a part – however big or small.

Now, go through the list and check off all the people whom you have explicitly thanked. Even a simple 'thank you' email is fine. If you have checked off everyone in the list, every last person that you added in those final two minutes, then it's hats off to you! Take a moment and soak in the gratitude that you have expressed to those surrounding you.

In most cases, I've found that when doing this exercise with people, more than 50% of the people in the list are not checked off. Meaning, people have not taken the time to thank those who played a role in their win.

Your mission, should you choose to accept it, is to send one more 'thank you' note to someone who have not been thanked already and thus checked off from the 'thank you' list. Here's the kicker, you need to do it today. You can even stop now and write and e-mail a 'thank you' note to this person. Let them know how much you appreciate their support and send the e-mail or put it in the mail today. Then, if you want bonus points, keep sending a 'thank you' note a day until you check off everyone in the list. Two per day if you're feeling inspired!

There would be no positive self-discovery if I simply told you every single reason why this would work, so please try and find it out for yourself. But I will give you a few reasons to get you started.

In general, people over-estimate what they brought to the table for a win and underestimate what others and luck brought to the table.

Performing this exercise for every significant win will bring out a list of people that either slipped your mind or you might have taken for granted. Do this exercise regularly and soon you will build the awareness that will enable you to stop taking many things for granted. In addition, you will start to realize and appreciate all the blessings around you.

This concept was originally published on LinkedIn. My friend, Dilip Saraf's comment there is very insightful. I have reproduced that here below:

"What I find is that merely a 'thank you' is often not enough. What most people miss in their message is being specific, personal and timely. For example, to you I'd write: "Thanks, Raj, for this reminder! I went through the list and just realized a number of people I had ignored in expressing my gratitude to them when what they did selflessly made a BIG difference in MY life! Now I feel complete. You are a good friend to have!"

It may just be "one more" thank you for you. But, it can still make an impact on the recipient of that thank you.

"*Silent gratitude isn't very much to anyone.*"

*- Gertrude Stein*

# Too Busy to Say Thank You

Everyone is very busy these days. Some people are so busy that they don't take the time to say a heartfelt 'thank you' for whatever gifts they receive.

If you are one of those very busy people, I hope you also know that some of that 'busy' is your own making.

Let us think about why you might be very busy.

**You get busy when you are paying attention to something.**
You pay attention to something if it is meaningful to you or it's meaningful to someone or something that matters to you. Possibly a cause you feel deeply about or an activity that you really enjoy. At least, that's how it should be most of the time.

Another reason may be you are bombarded with information from dozens of channels, speaking even beyond those that we physically interact with. You likely have multiple social media channels and e-mail in-boxes staking a claim for something that's precious and limited - your mindshare. These channels are robbing you of your precious time and insisting that they are important when they are simply time wasters. The majority of people are sadly the willing victims of such robbery every single day. Much of this initiated by our actions.

Used without caution, social media can become an addiction of the wrong kind. We get addicted to the ability to "broadcast" any and everything on our social media channels that will most likely receive instant feedback of some kind. This gives us the signal that every post is important. Otherwise, why would people engage with that content, right? We train ourselves to become addicted to our social media channels for affirmation and validation.

Let's explore another example for being so addicted to the social media channels: You post about something trivial. For example, let's say you post about you having a coffee on a rainy day. After posting, you move on to take care of more important things such as working on your personal or professional projects. After a brief amount of time, you likely take a break from your meaningful project to see if anyone interacted with your post even though it was simply sharing a small happening. We have been trained to focus on every engagement even with our daily and sometimes mundane activity to find affirmation. We spend hours upon hours trolling social media feeds reading information that is not as important as your meaningful personal or professional projects that you put on pause to engage in social media.

Add a series of such instances and you have easily lost hours of productive time in a workweek. The sad part is that you don't even notice it because you are labeling these lost hours as "engaging with social media." In reality, you are probably entertaining yourself in the name of engagement.

Social Media when used right has many benefits. However, the lazy option is to use it in a way where you get a false sense of being on the center stage for brief moments. Like many addictions, once you get that feeling you build a habit of want more. Soon, you are sucked into the activity so much that it is now a part of your second nature.

The result?

At some point, something's got to give and that something happens to be the important stuff in life. Whether it be your projects, developing a sense of being grateful for your blessings or you not having time to thank those who have made a difference in your life, there is a price to pay.

The good part is that you CAN change.

It starts with being aware or becoming aware that not all kinds of attention are important.

It starts by reflecting on what may be the hidden payoff you might be getting by engaging in trivial pursuits rather than working hard to contribute and add value.

It starts with you making a decision to get away from busy work to start doing smart work.

It starts with YOU are responsible for the consequences of any and all actions.

It starts with realizing that while there may be no short-term negative effects of unproductive behavior, that kind of behaviour will never help you in the long run.

It might be tough to challenge your habits and where you spend your time.

Busy for the sake of being busy helps no one...including YOU!

"When a person does not have gratitude, something is missing in his or her humanity."

- Elie Wiesel

# The Price of Not Thinking Enough

Let's assume that you are busy like everyone else and you forgot to thank someone for a favor received. You make a mental note that you need to thank that person, adding it to an already lengthy to-do list and promising to do so when your time frees up a time.

One of the two things will happen.

1. You continue to be too busy and forget about saying 'thank you'.

2. You feel that it's too late and the time to say 'thank you' has passed.

Let's start with the second response: that you feel it's too late to say 'thank you'. That is definitely a myth. **It is never too late to thank someone.** You are doing a disservice to yourself if you are holding back on genuinely expressing your gratitude no matter how long ago the favor occurred.

Now, let's look at the first case: you are simply too busy and forget to thank someone. If someone has touched your heart, it is impossible to forget that.

Rather than simply telling you that it's important to thank people and you just need to make time and do it, lets look at the price you might pay for not thanking.

Here is the list:

1. **You may end up on a mental blacklist:** The person who extended the favor knows the effort he put in to help you. While not everyone expects you to reciprocate back, many people would expect appreciation for their effort and thoughtfulness in extending the favor. When they don't receive appreciation for their action you might wind up on their "mental blacklist". The effect of that is simple- your future requests, if any, will go into a "low priority" queue or simply get ignored.

2. **You may lose the license to make a future request:** Next time you want to ask a favor of that person you may remember that you didn't thank him last time. So, it might be embarrassing for you to go back again to the same person and ask the favor when you didn't thank him for the last one.

3. **You might undermine the favor and over-estimate your strengths:** One reason you might not thank someone is that you might think it did not take a lot of work on the person's part to extend the favor. This happens if you see things superficially. The person might have just made a phone call. You can look at the action and think it is simply a phone call or you could think about all the real effort it could have caused that person to make that call. When you underestimate the effort the other person has made, there is a chance that you will over-estimate your own strengths. You may start to see things through your own capacity to perform that action which can lead to a self-centered view of things and decreases your focus on gratitude. Making this mistake can hurt you big time in the future.

4. **You may feel guilty (rightly so) for not saying thank you:** You know you should have thanked and you know that you didn't. That guilt can simply eat you from inside.

5. **It could reflect badly on you:** In some cases it might be so clear that you should have said 'thank you' and everyone around you knows that. In those situations, people can quickly make an assessment about your character.

6. **You might start getting used to taking people for granted:** This is the most dangerous way of paying a price for not thanking enough. Nobody likes to be taken for granted. In the long run, you will pay a big price for making this habit your second nature.

I can go on, but the point is simple – the right thing to do is to extend thanks to anyone and everyone who extends a favor to you. The alternate option is to pay a price now and pay a price in the future as well. The choice is yours.

> "*Gratitude is a duty which ought to be paid, but which none have a right to expect.*"
>
> *- Jean-Jacques Rousseau*

# Not Too Busy to Say Thank You

I have been a long time fan and friend of Sally Hogshead. She posted a short and touching story on Facebook about being grateful.

The photo and the story are below:

30 years ago, a man fell out of a tree stand and broke his back. He was paralyzed. My Dad, an orthopedic surgeon, set the

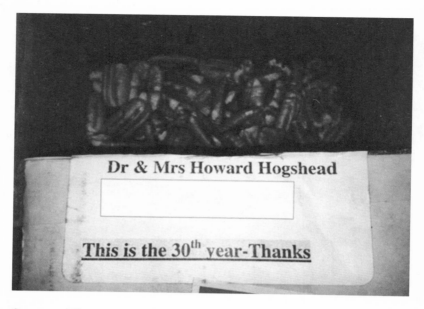

**Dr & Mrs Howard Hogshead**

**This is the 30<sup>th</sup> year-Thanks**

fracture. The man made a 100% recovery. Every year, he sends our family a box of pecans. This is the 30th year."

The story is short and it can get lost in the social media jungle. It's an important story with a brilliant lesson in it. So, I asked Sally's permission to re-tell the story and the lesson in this book.

Think about it. Sally's dad, Dr. Howard Hogshead, gave this person a life-changing gift. In fact, he almost handed over the man a new life.

How long should the person be grateful to Dr. Hogshead?

Simple – for the rest of his life!

That is exactly what he is showcasing by faithfully sending the thoughtful gift to the Hogshead family every single year since his injury. Imagine the smiles that this present brings, year after year, upon its arrival.

Think about your own life. It may not be as dramatic as the story highlighted above, but you can surely think of dozens of people who have given you life-changing gifts that have changed the trajectory of your life in ways that you had not imagined before. The question to reflect upon is – "Are you showing those kind souls a lifetime of gratefulness?"

The key takeaway to remember on this day and every day thereafter:

**Life changing gifts deserve a lifetime of gratefulness!**

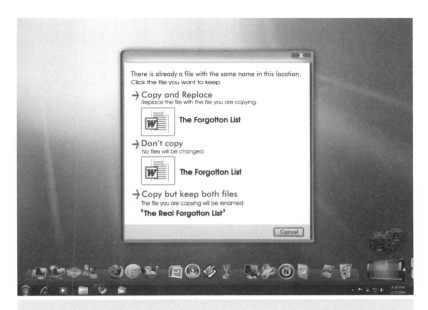

"*Sometimes we focus so much on what we don't have that we fail to see, appreciate and use what we do have.*"

*- Jeff Dixon*

# The Forgotten List

"My head hurts just thinking about it," confessed my friend. "I really can't believe it. I have helped literally hundreds of people when they were nobody. Now, most of them have succeeded in life. Very few people remember what help I provided them and sadly, most of them seem to have completely forgotten the fact that I played a reasonably important role in making them who they are today."

# The Forgotten List

_____

_____

_____

_____

_____

_____

_____

_____

Yes, there is a name for such a list "The Forgotten List". It is the list of people that you have helped to get to where they are today and are not willing to acknowledge or reciprocate in any way. You contributed your mind share, network, knowledge, time and/or resources to move the needle for them. Now that they don't need you anymore they conveniently forgot about what they received from you in the past. You helped them to get moving and once they got a start they simply moved on.

The truth of the matter is that this hurts you. If you can relate to this feeling, remember that you are not alone. There are hundreds and thousands of people out there who share your pain and silent suffering. We all wish the situation were different.

Actually, the real problem is not that the forgotten list is too long but it is your expectation that the situation should be different from what it is. Like everything else in life the 80-20 rule applies here also. Of the people whom you helped, 80% will forget your help or take it for granted. These are the people who are on The Forgotten List. Then, there are 20% of those that will want to reciprocate in some way. If you want to increase the 20% of people who don't make it on The Forgotten List line, you can't focus on the people that are already on that list. Simply do your best to increase the help you offer to people. If you increase this 20% of people that you extend help to and who reciprocate thanks, then by default, you are decreasing the percent of people that fall into The Forgotten List.

There is an even bigger problem at play when you are busy judging and categorizing all the people who have helped you. That problem is the growing **The Real Forgotten List**.

**The Real Forgotten List**

The Real Forgotten List is similar to The Forgotten List. It is the list of people who have helped and shaped you to become who YOU are today and you have conveniently forgotten them because <enter your reason(s) here>.

This is where you step down from the bench and take the witness stand.

This is where you look at the mirror and start judging yourself.

This is where the rubber meets the road.

This is where you move away from the comfort of judging others to the discomfort of reflecting on yourself.

This is where you give credit where it's due.

This is where you acknowledge that YOU are part of the problem you are accusing others to be guilty of.

There is Still Time.

If The Real Forgotten List shook you even a tiny bit know that it's never too late to make amends. The Grateful Project (in the next chapter) is a good place to start, but the real change

happens when you start being mindful of even the smallest of help people provide on a day-to-day basis. You and I are terribly insufficient on our own to be and do what it takes to lead a meaningful life. So, it's
guaranteed that we are being blessed by good help.

The question is, "when will you start noticing and acknowledging all these blessings?"

*"... my obsession with gratefulness. I can't stop. Just now, I press the elevator button and am thankful that it arrives quickly. I get onto the elevator and am thankful that the elevator cable didn't snap and plummet me to the basement. I go to the fifth floor and am thankful that I didn't have to stop on the second or third or fourth floor. I get out and am thankful that Julie left the door unlocked so I don't have to rummage for my King Kong key ring. I walk in, and am thankful that Jasper is home and healthy and stuffing his face with pineapple wedges. And on, and on. I'm actually muttering to myself, 'Thank you. . .thank you. . . thank you.' It's an odd way to live. But also kind of great and powerful. I've never before been so aware of the thousands of little good things, the thousands of things that go right every day."*

*- A.J. Jacobs*
*The Year of Living Biblically: One Man's*
*Humble Quest to Follow the Bible as Literally as Possible*

# The Grateful Project

Note to the reader:  there are two ways to read this chapter. The first is to read it as a way to engage in intellectual entertainment. The second is to reflect thoughtfully and explore whether it makes a difference.

How you read this chapter is your choice, but it's important to know which of the two ways you take to approach this information.

The foundation for this chapter was inspired by Stoic Philosophy. Don't worry – you don't need to be an expert in stoicism to understand the concept outlined in the chapter.

I have used The Grateful Project exercise many times over my years of consulting and speaking. While the reactions have been varied, one thing has been clear. The returns that people receive through this exercise are directly tied to the effort and reflection they put in into answering the questions.

The Grateful Project is all about what the name says. It's all about gratitude. The entire exercise usually takes about 30 minutes.

## Part 1: THEM (15 minutes)

Part 1 is all about "them", those that shaped your life.

## 1. YESTERDAY

> Think back to last night. Assume that yesterday was your last day on earth. Your mission, if you chose to accept it, was to list as many names as possible of the people for whom you are grateful. Anyone that touched you in some meaningful way that shaped your life to be who you became was to be added to the list. Anyone who taught a life lesson that changed the trajectory of your life for the better were added to the list. Take ten minutes to get as many names as possible. This is the first list.

## 2. TODAY

Let us assume that you got a one bonus day. Today, your goal is simply to focus on the delta, meaning that your list will now contain only those people that touched your life in a meaningful way today. The goal is to list as many people as possible. Take the next five minutes to list as many as possible. This is the second list.

### Part 2: "YOU" (15 minutes)

Part 2 is all about you, the lives that you shaped in some meaningful way.

### 1. TODAY

Again, image that today is your last day. Imagine all the people who you have touched in any way (good, bad and ugly) are doing this exercise. How many will put you on the first list? Take ten minutes to do this exercise. This is the third list.

### 2. TOMORROW

Now, imagine that you got that bonus day and you have all of tomorrow. Think of the people that you included in the list above and envision that they are doing the same exercise you are. All the people who you will touch tomorrow are involved in this exercise. How many of those people will chose to include you in the second list? Take five minutes to do this exercise. This is the fourth list.

Now, think about your real tomorrow. Think what changes you will make in the way you will live and interact with whomever you will touch tomorrow?

## A Request

If this exercise has touched you in a meaningful way send this book, after you read it of course, to one of the people in the first list. Include a 'thank you' note and make their day.

# The REAL Golden Network

There is a network of people you should be eternally grateful for and they are part of your REAL golden network.

Let me explain.

If you are going for a hike on a hill close to your home you might be able to safely complete the hike on your own. However, if your goal is to climb Mount Everest you need to train with people who know how to hike a mountain like that. When your training is complete and the time has come to climb, you need someone to guide you and a team to hike with that will help you along the trail.

Positioning yourself with the right network provides you an advantage. You can accomplish much more because you are not alone. When you are part of the right network, you equally contribute what you can to everyone in the group as the other members do. To summarize this though - the right network can help you accomplish more.

Now, that's a good background for me to make a point.

But, before that, let me share a couple of conversations in the last few weeks:

## Two Conversations

The first conversation was with a long-time friend. We were catching up on each other's lives. My friend didn't understand one of my business decisions and asked me to explain. I explained my rationale and he listened then shared another way of looking at the same situation. We started discussing the topic and before we knew it we were deep into a brainstorming session on the topic. I realized that by talking about the idea together we arrived at something far better than what I could have done on my own. More importantly, I realized that I had added to my repository of worldviews and expanded my thought patterns just with one discussion.

The second conversation was with one of my mentors. We were discussing one of my new projects and I was very proud to share what I had come up with so far. Within a few minutes of talking, my mentor challenged me to think about repurposing what I had created to get a lot more continual value. My mentor had not just helped me with this opportunity but had provided me a new way to look at any such opportunity in the future.

What was the common thread between the two conversations? It was the conversation's ability to change how I think about something and make me "better" and increase my capacity to think better,

## Harnessing the Power of the Real Golden Network

The real golden network is one where you become a better person, through better thinking, as a result of having conversations with the members of that network. It's a network of similar thinkers that you invest and build over the years. It could even be a club where you pay a fee and become a member. The general term for such a club is called a mastermind group.

Here are three things to remember as you engage this network:

### 1. The added benefit.

You don't initiate, build and nurture these networks because you will benefit from them. When you belong to a network like this it's filled with that already make your life very special. It's simply an added value that this network can have additional benefits. Once you understand this at the deepest level you will start respecting the network in a whole different way.

### 2. Being vulnerable.

This is not a network where you wear your act like superman and behave like you are invincible. You may want to keep that image for one of those PR stunts because you won't need it here. In fact, you need to have the exact opposite attitude- one of vulnerability. You need to bring the real "you" to participate in this network, by contributing and finding value.

### 3. Fulfilling obligations.

What this network gives you, more than anything, is the gift of a new way of thinking. You are the best judge to put a value that new thinking brings to you. Every such gift you receive from this network will create a future obligation for you. It is your responsibility to fulfill it without fail.

If you don't have a real golden network, go ahead and start building one. If you do have a real golden network, be grateful for being a part of it.

*"No duty is more urgent than that of returning thanks"*

*- James Allen*

# Thank Powerfully

We have established that an attitude of gratitude is an important factor in personal growth. You might remember your parents telling you from the time you were young to be thankful to those who help you.

As we talked earlier, and established through the exercises, you are where you are today because of many people who helped you get here. It can sometimes be easy to forget the people who helped you. You might think that most of your success is because you are smart and worked hard. Of course, you'd admit that there was a little help here and there. This is where most people are wrong. The reality is that we are not as smart as we think we are, and, we underestimate the help we had along the way to get where we are today.

As we previously learned, the first step is to recognize the real contribution of people around you and to thank them. There are many ways to thank people. It might be as simple as sending a 'thank you' email or sending them a gift card. Perhaps it could even be sending flowers, taking them to lunch or coffee or even picking up the phone and calling and thanking them. The list goes on. There are thousands of ways to thank someone- some are easier and some are difficult. Some approaches might cost you nothing except your time and some other approaches might cost you a fortune. What matters most is that you put even a few minutes of thought into finding a genuine way to express your gratitude.

Think about it.

The best way to thank someone is to help them with what matters most to them **without adding additional cost** for them to receive that help. To put it simply, do something that will enrich their lives and make a meaningful impact for them.

People are busy and they typically have more on their plate than they can get done. However powerful they are, many people would like to admit that they too could use some help with their projects. They help others but they also take on challenges beyond their current capacity. You have a great opportunity to figure out how you can add value to someone else's life in a meaningful way.

Go ahead, think of someone that you can thank today and **do it in a powerful way.**

"*It is a sign of mediocrity when you express gratitude with moderation.*"

*- Roberto Benigni*

# Re-labeling Your Way to Grateful Living

Throughout this book, we have talked about two sides of a scale. The first is cultivating a lifestyle of being grateful on one end of the spectrum, and on the other is a lifestyle of taking people and things for granted. You might wonder why would anyone want to be on the side that takes people for granted?

While there are many reasons, let's cover a few:

## 1. Thoughtless Media Consumption.

Each day, you are overwhelmed with advertisements from the time we wake up to the time we go to bed. Let's think about the fundamental premise of an ad which is to sell a product or service. The point of an ad is to create a level of discontent with your current situation and explain how this product or service will change and enrich your life. There are hundreds, if not thousands, of ads that we see per day.

Since we are exposed to literally hundreds of ads throughout the day some narratives are bound to catch your attention. Once that happens you start to shift your focus to a growing discontent and the quest to quell it rather than focusing on gratitude for both what and who you already have in your life.

## 2. Social Media Makes it More Complex.

We talked about social media but it's worth revisiting that topic again.

Social media (e.g.,: Facebook, Twitter, Instagram) is a place where people surface their "best moments of life" in general. If you have a thousand friends, you can safely assume that at least ten of them will be celebrating something on a particular day (a party, traveling, an achievement, etc.) and they will post their celebratory photographs to share those moments. Tomorrow comes and ten other people in your circle may be celebrating something else. The same logic applies for day after tomorrow.

The problem?

If you lose perspective you can easily assume that every day a large part of your network is celebrating something or the other and for some reason God left you out of the always-on-party in this world.

Again, when the focus shifts to ask "Why me?" or "Why not

me?" it is hard to pay attention to things and people in your life that are to be grateful for.

## 3. Convenience

You may have a hard time admitting this but there is convenience in taking people for granted. It's not right in anyway but it's sure convenient.

## Rule Applies Everywhere

Bad things happen to good people too. We are victims of circumstance at times. If that is 20% of the time, it can't bring your mood down 80% of the time.

## Re-labeling: Gifts or Lessons

What if you start re-labeling everything and everyone around you as a gift or a lesson?

Imagine living everyday either welcoming those gifts or learning from the lessons.

Actually, let's look at it the other way, what if you don't?

When you don't follow the "gifts or lessons" mental model, you will start seeing more problems, issues, concerns and roadblocks. You easily go down a rabbit hole of finding who's to blame for what's happening to you. When the entire focus is looking at what's wrong in life where is the time to notice and acknowledge the dozens of gifts that are coming your way every day, let alone have time to be thankful and extend thanks?

Let's assume that the 80-20 rule is at play and we are focusing on 80% of the situations. You have only two labels with which to view the situation:

1. A Gift.

2. A Lesson.

You are forced to assign one of these two labels to the situation. Try this for a few days and you will notice that you are starting to notice gifts more often and you are learning a lot more. This magic happens because of the power of the moods. The gift or the lesson label will automatically set you up in a celebratory mood or in the mood of wonder.

# Taking Action

*"Gratitude helps you to grow and expand; gratitude brings joy and laughter into your lives and into the lives of all those around you."*

*- Eileen Caddy*

You can't read the mind of anyone else. Someone else cannot read your mind either. There is no current technology that can deliver your "grateful" feelings to someone. You still have to do it the old-fashioned way. There are no shortcuts available!

The only way forward is to take action.

We discussed about how to thank powerfully by making a difference in what matters most to them without adding additional cost to receive that help.

It is easier said than done but nothing good is rarely easy anyway.

Begin with *YOUR HEART*
with **RIGHT**
INTENTION

"*Be kind whenever possible... It is always possible.*"

*- The Dalai Lama*

# The Magic Begins With the Right Intention

There is a very slight chance that you might think what additional benefit you might get by thanking someone. Before you answer that question - stop for a second and question that question. If this question still lingers in your mind there is a good chance that you skipped reading the first section. If yes, take a few minutes to read or re-read the first section about shifting the mindset.

The magic is in the intention. You might wear a mask in your everyday life. The mask may be able to hide a few things but it can rarely hide your intentions because they are loud and clear through your words and actions.

Your intention has to be to contribute and without that all bets are off. I am not suggesting that you should not consume but the equation has to be that your contribution has to be far greater than your consumption.

> *"The world needs more demonstration than it needs instruction."*
>
> *- Wallace D. Wattles*

# Get Started

You can of course get started with a simple card. There are eight ready to send "Thank You" included in this book. All you need is to decide who you need to send this to and get going.

All the best!